On the Origin of Free-Masonry

Posthumous Work

By

Thomas Paine

Published by Forgotten Books 2012

Originally Published 1810

PIBN 1000049320

ON THE

ORIGIN

OF

FREE-MASONRY.

....

BY THOMAS PAINE.

....

POSTHUMOUS WORK.

NEW-YORK:

PRINTED AND SOLD BY ELLIOT AND CRISSY,

NO. 114 WATER-STREET.

1810.

ORIGIN

OF

FREE-MASONRY.

IT is always understood that Free-Masons have a secret which they carefully conceal; but from every thing that can be collected from their own accounts of Masonry their real secret is no other than their origin, which but few of them understand; and those who do, envelope it in mystery.

The society of Masons are distinguished into three classes or degrees. 1st, the Entered Apprentice. 2d, the Fellow Craft. 3d, the Master-Mason.

The entered apprentice knows but little more of Masonry than the use of signs and tokens, and certain steps and words, by which Masons can recognise each other, without being discovered by a person who is not a mason. The fellow-craft is not much better instructed in masonry than the entered apprentice. It is only in the Master-Mason's Lodge that whatever knowledge remains of the origin of masonry is preserved and concealed.

In 1730, Samuel Pritchard, member of a constituted lodge in England, published a treatise entitled *Masonry Dissected;* and made oath before the Lord Mayor of London that it was a true copy.

Samuel Pritchard maketh oath that the copy hereunto annexed is a true and genuine copy in every particular.

In his work he has given the catechism, or examination in question and answer, of the apprentice, the fellow-craft and the Master Mason. There was no difficulty in his doing this as it is mere form. . .

In his introduction he says, " The original institution of masonry consisted in the foundation of the liberal arts and sciences, but more especially on Geometry; for at the building of the Tower of Babel the art and mystery of Masonry was first introduced, and from thence handed down by *Euclid*, a worthy and excellent Mathematician of the Egyptians; and he communicated it to *Hiram*, the Master Mason concerned in building Solomon's Temple in Jerusalem."

Besides the absurdity of deriving masonry from the building of Babel, where, according to the story, the confusion of languages prevented builders understanding each other, and consequently of communicating any knowledge they had, there is a glaring contradiction in point of chronology in the account he gives.

Solomon's Temple was built and dedicated 1004 years before the christian era; and *Euclid*, as may be seen in the tables of chronology, lived 277 years before the same era. It was therefore impossible that Euclid could communicate any thing to Hiram, since Euclid did not live till 700 years after the time of Hiram.

In 1783 captain George Smith, inspector of the Royal Artillery Academy, at Woolwich, in England, and Provincial Grand Master of Masonry for the county of Kent, published a treatise entitled The Use and Abuse of Free-Masonry.

In his chapter of the antiquity of masonry he makes it to be coeval with creation, " When, says he, the sovereign architect raised on masonic principles, the beauteous globe, and commanded that master science, Geometry, to lay the planetary world, and to regulate by its laws the whole stupendous system in just unerring proportion, rolling round the central sun."

" But, continues he, I am not at liberty publicly to undraw the curtain, and openly to des-
cant on this head, it is sacred, and ever will
remain so; those who are honoured with the
trust will not reveal it, and those who are ignorant of it cannot betray it." By this last part of
the phrase, Smith means the two inferior classes,
the fellow-craft and the entered apprentice, for
he says in the next page of his work, " It is not
every one that is barely initiated into Free-Masonry that is entrusted with all the mysteries
thereto belonging; they are not attainable as
things of course, nor by every capacity."

The learned but unfortunate Doctor Dodd,
Grand Chaplain of Masonry, in his oration at
the dedication of Free-Mason's Hall, London,
traces Masonry through a variety of stages.
Masons, says he, are well informed from their
own private and interior records that the building of Solomon's Temple is an important era,
from whence they derive many mysteries of their
art. " Now, says he, be it remembered that this

great event took place above 1000 years before the Christian era, and consequently more than a century before Homer, the first of the Grecian Poets, wrote; and above five centuries before Pythagoras brought from the east his sublime system of truly masonic instruction to illuminate our western world.

" But remote as this period is, we date not from thence the commencement of our art. For though it might owe to the wise and glorious King of Israel, some of its many mystic forms and hieroglyphic ceremonies, yet certainly the art itself is coeval with man, the great subject of it.

" We trace, continues he, its footsteps in the most distant, the most remote ages and nations of the world. We find it among the first and most celebrated civilizers of the East. We deduce it regularly from the first astronomers on the plains of Chaldea, to the wise and mystic kings and priests of Egypt, the sages of Greece, and the philosophers of Rome."

From these reports and declarations of Masons of the highest order in the institution, we see that Masonry, without publicly declaring so, lays claim to some divine communication from the creator in a manner different from, and unconnected with, the book which the christians call the bible; and the natural result from this is, that Masonry is derived from some very ancient religion wholly independent of, and unconnected with that book.

To come then at once to the point, *Masonry* (as I shall shew from the customs, ceremonies, hieroglyphics and chronology of Masonry) is derived, and is the remains of, the religion of the ancient Druids; who like the magi of Persia and the priests of Heliopolis in Egypt, were Priests of the Sun. They paid worship to this great luminary, as the great visible agent of a great invisible first cause, whom they styled. time without limits.

In Masonry many of the ceremonies of the

B

Druids are preserved in their original state, at least without any parody. With them the sun is still the sun; and his image, in the form of the sun, is the great emblematical ornament of Masonic Lodges and Masonic dresses. It is the central figure on their aprons, and they wear it also pendant on the breast in their lodges and in their processions.

At what period of antiquity, or in what nation, this religion was first established, is lost in the labyrinth of unrecorded times. It is generally ascribed to the ancient Egyptians, the Babylonians and Chaldeans, and reduced afterwards to a system regulated by the apparent progress of the sun through the 12 signs of the Zodiac by Zoroaster the law-giver of Persia, from whence Pythagoras brought it into Greece. It is to these matters Dr. Dodd refers in the passage already quoted from his oration.

The worship of the sun as the great visible agent of a great invisible first cause, time without limits, spread itself over a considerable part of Asia and Africa, from thence to Greece and Rome, through all ancient Gaul and into Britain and Ireland.

Smith, in his chapter on the Antiquity of Masonry in Britain, says, that, " Notwithstanding the obscurity which envelopes Masonic history in that country, various circumstances contribute to prove that Free-Masonry was introduced into Britain about 1030 years before Christ."

It cannot be Masonry in its present state that Smith here alludes to. The Druids flourished in Britain at the period he speaks of, and it is from them that Masonry is descended. Smith has put the child in the place of the parent.

It sometimes happens as well in writing as in conversation that a person lets slip an expression that serves to unravel what he intends to conceal, and this is the case with Smith, for in the same

chapter he says, " The Druids, when they com-
mitted any thing to writing, used the Greek al-
phabet, and I am bold to assert that the most per-
fect remains of the Druids' rites and ceremonies
are preserved in the customs and ceremonies of
the Masons that are to be found existing among
mankind. My brethren, says he, may be able
to trace them with greater exactness than I am
at liberty to explain to the public."

This is a confession from a Master Mason,
without intending it to be so understood by the
public, that Masonry is the remains of the religion of the Druids; the reason for the Masons
keeping this a secret I shall explain in the course
of this work.

As the study and contemplation of the Creator
in the works of the creation of which the sun as
the great visible agent of that Being, was the
visible object of the adoration of Druids, all
their religious rites and ceremonies had reference to the apparent progress of the sun through

the twelve signs of the Zodiac, and his influence upon the earth. The Masons adopt the same practices. The roof of their Temples or Lodges is ornamented with a sun, and the floor is a representation of the variegated face of the earth, either by carpeting or Mosaic Work.

Free Masons Hall, in great Queen-street, Lincolns Inn fields, London, is a magnificent building, and cost upwards of 12,000 pounds sterling. Smith, in speaking of this building says (page 152) ' The roof of this magnificent Hall is, in all probability the highest piece of finished architecture in Europe. In the center of this roof, a most resplendent sun is represented in burnished gold, surrounded with the 12 signs of the Zodiac with their respective characters:

Aries ♈.	Libra ♎.
Taurus ♉.	Scorpio ♏.
Gemini ♊.	Sagittarius ♐.
Cancer ♋.	Capricornus ♑.
Leo ♌.	Aquarius ♒.
Virgo ♍.	Pisces ♓.

" After giving this description he says, " The emblematical meaning of the sun is well known to the enlightened and inquisitive Free-Mason; and as the real sun is situated in the center of the universe, so the emblematical sun is the center of real Masonry. We all know, continues he, that the sun is the fountain of light, the source of the seasons, the cause of the vicissitudes of day and night, the parent of vegetation, the friend of man; hence the scientific Free-Mason only knows the reason why the sun is placed in the center of this beautiful hall.''

The masons, in order to protect themselves from the persecution of the christian church, have always spoken in a mystical manner of the figure of the sun in their lodges, or, like the astronomer Lalande, who is a mason, been silent upon the subject.

The Lodges of the Masons, if built for the purpose, are constructed in a manner to correspond with the apparent motion of the sun. They are situated East and West. The Master's place is always in the East. In the examination of an Entered Apprentice, the Master, among many other questions asks him,

Q.   How is the Lodge situated?

A.   East and West.

Q.   Why so?

A.   Because all churches and chapels are or ought to be so.

This answer, which is mere catechismal form, is not an answer to the question. It does no more than remove the question a point further, which is, why ought all churches and chapels to be so? But as the Entered Apprentice is not initiated into the druidical mysteries of Masonry, he is not asked any questions to which a direct answer would lead thereto.

Q.   Where stands your Master?

A.   In the East.

Q.   Why so?

A.   As the sun rises in the East and opens the day, so the Master stands in the East (with his right hand upon his left breast, being a sign, and the square about his neck) to open the lodge and set his men at work.

Q. Where stand your Wardens?

A. In the West.

Q. What is their business?

A. As the sun sets in the West to close the day, so the Wardens stand in the west (with their right hands upon their left breasts, being a sign, and the level and plumb, rule about their necks) to close the lodge, and dismiss the men from labour, paying them their wages.

Here the name of the sun is mentioned, but it is proper to observe, that in this place it has reference only to labour or to the time of labour, and not to any religious druidical rite or ceremony, as it would have with respect to the situation of Lodges East and West. I have already observed in the chapter on the origin of the christian religion, that the situation of churches East and West is taken from the worship of the sun which rises in the East. The christians never bury their dead on the north side of a church; and a Mason's Lodge always has, or is supposed to have, three windows, which are called fixed lights, to distinguish them from the moveable lights of the sun and the moon. The Master asks the Entered Apprentice

Q. How are they (the fixed lights) situated?

A. East, west, and south.

Q. What are their uses?

A. To light the men to and from their work.

Q. Why are there no lights in the North?

A. Because the sun darts no rays from thence.

This among numerous other instances shews that the christian religion and Masonry have one and the same common origin, the ancient worship of the sun.

The high festival of the masons is on the day they call St. John's day; but every enlightened mason must know that holding their festival on

C

this day has no reference to the person called St. John, and that it is only to disguise the true cause of holding it on this day, that they call the day by that name. As there were Masons, or at least Druids, many centuries before the time of St. John, if such person ever existed, the holding their festival on this day must refer to some cause totally unconnected with John.

The case is, that the day called St. John's day is the 24th of June, and is what is called *midsummer day*. The sun is then arrived at the summer solstice, and with respect to his meridional altitude, or height at high noon, appear for some days to be of the same height. The astronomical longest day, like the shortest day, is not every year, on account of leap year, on the same numerical day, and therefore the 24th of June is always taken for midsummer day; and it is in honour of the sun, which has then arrived at his greatest height in our hemisphere, and not any thing with respect to St. John, that this annual festival of the Masons, taken from the Druids, is celebrated on midsummer day.

Customs will often outlive the remembrance of their origin, and this is the case with respect to a custom still practised in Ireland, where the Druids flourished at the time they flourished in Britain.   On the eve of St. John's day, that is, on the eve of midsummer day, the Irish light fires on the tops of the hills.   This can have no reference to St. John; but it has emblematical reference to the sun which on that day is at his highest summer elevation, and might in common language be said to have arrived at the top of the hill.

As to what masons and books of masonry tell us of Solomon's Temple at Jerusalem, it is no ways improbable that some masonic ceremonies may have been derived from the building of that Temple, for the worship of the sun was in practice many centuries before the temple existed, or before the Israelites came out of Egypt.   And we learn from the history of the Jewish Kings, 2 Kings, chap. 22, 23, that the worship of the sun was performed by the Jews in that temple. It is, however, much to be doubted, if it was done with the same scientific purity and religious morality, with which it was performed by the Druids, who by all accounts that historically remain of them, were a wise, learned and moral class of men. The Jews, on the contrary, were ignorant of astronomy, and of science in general, and if a religion founded upon astronomy, fell into their hands, it is almost certain it would be corrupted. We do not read in the history of the Jews, whether in the bible or elsewhere, that they were the inventors or the improvers of any one art or science. Even in the building of this temple, the Jews did not know how to square and frame the timber for beginning and carrying on the work, and Solomon was obliged to send to Hiram, King of Tyre, (Zidon) to procure workmen; "*for thou knowest*, (says Solomon to Hiram) 1 Kings, chap. 5, v. 6) *that there is not among us any that can skill to hew timber like unto the Zidonians.''* This Temple was more properly Hiram's Temple than Solomon's, and if the Masons derive any thing from the building of it, they owe it to the Zidonians and not to the Jews.—But to return to the worship of the sun in this Temple.

It is said, 2 kings, chap. 23, v. 5, "and King Josiah put down all the Idolatrous priests that burned incence unto the sun, the moon, the planets and to all the host of heaven."—And it is said at the 11th v. " and he took away the horses that the kings of Judah had given to the sun at the entering in of the house of the Lord, and burned the chariots of the sun with fire, v. 13, and the high places that were before Jerusalem, which were on the right hand of the mount of corruption, which Solomon the king of Israel had builded for Astoreth, the abomination of the Zidonians (the very people that built the temple) did the king defile.

Besides these things, the description that

Josephus gives of the decorations of this Temple, resemble on a large scale, those of a Mason's Lodge. He says that the distribution of the several parts of the Temple of the Jews represented all nature, particularly the parts most apparent of it, as the sun, the moon, the planets, the zodiac, the earth, the elements, and that the system of the world was retraced there by numerous ingenious emblems. These, in all probability, are what Josiah, in his ignorance, calls the abomination of the Zidonians.* Every thing, however, drawn from this Temple† and

---

* Smith in speaking of a Lodge says, when the Lodge is revealed to an entering Mason, it discovers to him *a representation of the World;* in which from the wonders of nature we are led to contemplate her great original, and worship him from his mighty works; and we are thereby also moved to exercise those moral and social virtues which become mankind as the servants of the great Architect of the world.

† It may not be improper here to observe, that the law called the law of Moses, could not have been in existence at the time of building this Temple. Here is the likeness of things in heaven above, and in earth beneath. And we read in 1 Kings, chap. 6, 7. that Solomon made cherubs and cherubims, that he *carved* all the walls of the house round

applied to Masonry, still refers to the worship of the sun, however corrupted or misunderstood by the Jews, and consequently to the religion of the Druids.

Another circumstance which shews that Masonry is derived from some ancient system, prior to, and unconnected with, the christian religion, is the chronology, or method of counting time, used by the Masons in the records of their Lodges. They make no use of what is called the christian era, and they reckon their months numerically as the ancient Egyptians did, and as the Quakers do now. I have by me a record of a French Lodge at the time the late Duke of Orleans, then Duke de Chartres was Grand Master of Masonry in France. It begins as follows:

about with cherubims and palm-trees. and open flowers, and that he made a molten sea, placed on twelve oxen, and that the ledges of it were ornamented with lions, oxen and cherubims; all this is contrary to the law called the law of Moses.

" *Le trentieme jour du sixieme mois de l'an de la V. L. cinq mil septcent soixante treize* " that is, The thirtieth day of the sixth month of the year of the venerable Lodge, five thousand seven hundred and seventy-three. By what I observe in English books of Masonry, the English Masons use the initials A. L. and not V. L. By A. L. they mean in *the year of the Lodge*, as the christians by A. D. mean in the year of the Lord. But A. L. like V. L. refers to the same chronological era, that is, to the supposed time of the Creation.

Though the Masons have taken many of their ceremonies and hieroglyphics from the ancient Egyptians, it is certain they have not taken their chronology from thence. If they had, the church would soon have sent them to the stake; as the chronology of the Egyptians, like that of the Chinese, goes many thousand years beyond the bible chronology.

The religion of the Druids, as before said,

was the same as the religion of the ancient Egyptians. The priests of Egypt were the professors and teachers of science, and were styled priests of Heliopolis, that is, of the *city of the sun.* The Druids in Europe, who were the same order of men, have their name from the Teutonic or ancient German language; the Germans being anciently called Teutones. The word Druid signifies a *wise man.* In Persia they were called magi, which signifies the same thing.

" Egypt, says Smith, from whence we derive many of our mysteries, hath always borne a distinguished rank in history, and was once celebrated above all others for its antiquities, learning, opulence, and fertility. In their system, their principal hero-gods, Osiris and Isis, theologically represented the supreme Being and universal Nature; and physically, the two great celestial luminaries, the sun and the moon, by whose influence all nature was actuated. The experienced brethren of the society (says Smith in a note to this passage) are well informed what affinity these symbols bear to Masonry, and why they are used in all Masonic Lodges."

In speaking of the apparel of the Masons in their Lodges, part of which, as we see in their public processions, is a white leather apron, he says, " the Druids were apparelled in white at the time of their sacrifices and solemn offices. The Egyptian Priests of Osiris wore snow-white cotton. The Grecian and most other priests wore white garments. As Masons, we regard the principles of those *who were the first worshippers of the true God*, imitate their apparel, and assume the badge of innocence.

" The Egyptians, continues Smith, in the earliest ages, constituted a great number of Lodges, but with assiduous care kept their secrets of Masonry from all strangers. These secrets have been imperfectly handed down to us by oral tradition only, and ought to be kept undiscovered to the labourers, crafts-men, and apprentices, till by good behaviour, and long

study, they become better acquainted in Geometry and the liberal arts, and thereby qualified
for Masters and Wardens, which is seldom or
ever the case with English Masons."

Under the head of Free-Masonry, written by
the astronomer Lalande, in the French Encyclo-
pedia, I expected from his great knowledge in
astronomy, to have found much information on
the origin of Masonry; for what connection can
there be between any institution and the sun and
twelve signs of the Zodiac, if there be not some-
thing in that institution, or in its origin, that has
reference to astronomy. Every thing used as an
hieroglyphic, has reference to the subject and
purpose for which it is used; and we are not to
suppose the Free-Masons, among whom are
many very learned and scientific men, to be such
idiots as to make use of astronomical signs without some astronomical purpose.

But I was much disappointed in my expecta-
tion from Lalande. In speaking of the origin of

Masonry, he says " *L'origine de la maçonerie se perd, comme tant d'autres, dans l'obscurite des temps;*" that is, the origin of masonry, like many others, loses itself in the obscurity of time. When I came to this expression, I supposed Lalande a Mason, and on enquiry found he was. This *passing over* saved him from the embarrassment which Masons are under respecting the disclosure of their origin, and which they are sworn to conceal. There is a society of Masons in Dublin who take the name of Druids; these Masons must be supposed to have a reason for taking that name.

I come now to speak of the cause of secresy used by the Masons.

The natural source of secresy is fear. When any new religion over-runs a former religion, the professors of the new become the persecutors of the old. We see this in all the instances that history brings before us. When Hilkiah the Priest and Shaphan the scribe, in the reign of king Josiah, found, or pretended to find, the law, called the law of Moses, a thousand years after the time of Moses, and it does not appear from the 2d Book of Kings, chapters 22, 23, that such law was ever practised or known before the time of Josiah; he established that law as a national religion, and put all the priests of the sun to death. When the christian religion over-ran the Jewish religion, the Jews were the continual subject of persecution in all christian countries. When the Protestant religion in England over-ran the Roman Catholic religion, it was made death for a catholic priest to be found in England. As this has been the case in all the instances we have any knowledge of, we are obliged to admit it with respect to the case in question, and that when the christian religion over-ran the religion of the Druids in Italy, ancient Gaul, Britain, and Ireland, the Druids became the subject of persecution. This would naturally and necessarily oblige such of them as remained attached to their original religion to meet in secret and under the strongest injunctions of secresy. Their safety depended upon it. A false brother might expose the lives of many of them to destruction; and from the remains of the religion of the Druids, thus preserved, arose the institution which, to avoid the name of Druid, took that of Mason, and practised, under this new name, the rights and ceremonies of Druids.

F I N I S.